EMMANUEL JOSEPH

Blueprint of Influence, Navigating the Intersection of Politics, Culture, and Commerce

Copyright © 2025 by Emmanuel Joseph

All rights reserved. No part of this publication may be reproduced, stored or transmitted in any form or by any means, electronic, mechanical, photocopying, recording, scanning, or otherwise without written permission from the publisher. It is illegal to copy this book, post it to a website, or distribute it by any other means without permission.

First edition

*This book was professionally typeset on Reedsy.
Find out more at reedsy.com*

Contents

1 Chapter 1   1
2 Chapter 15: The Power of Networks   16
3 Chapter 16: The Art of Negotiation   18
4 Chapter 17: The Legacy of Influence   20

1

Chapter 1

Chapter 1: The Foundations of Influence Influence is a powerful tool that has been wielded by leaders, thinkers, and changemakers throughout history. It is the ability to shape opinions, behaviors, and decisions in a way that aligns with a particular vision or goal. At its core, influence is about communication and connection. It involves understanding the needs and desires of others and crafting messages that resonate with them. Successful influencers are those who can build trust, inspire action, and create a sense of community around their ideas.

The foundations of influence are rooted in several key principles. First, credibility is essential. People are more likely to be persuaded by those they perceive as knowledgeable, honest, and reliable. Building credibility involves demonstrating expertise, being transparent, and consistently delivering on promises. Second, emotional appeal plays a crucial role. Influencers who can tap into the emotions of their audience—whether through storytelling, empathy, or passion—can create a deeper connection and motivate action. Finally, social proof, or the validation of an idea by others, is a powerful driver of influence. When people see that others support a particular viewpoint, they are more likely to adopt it themselves.

In today's interconnected world, the reach of influence has expanded dramatically. Social media platforms, for instance, allow individuals to share their ideas with a global audience instantly. This democratization of influence means that anyone with a compelling message and the right strategies can become a powerful force for change. However, it also means that the competition for attention is fierce, and the ability to stand out and be heard is more challenging than ever.

Navigating the intersection of politics, culture, and commerce requires a nuanced understanding of how influence operates in these different spheres. Political influencers must consider the diverse and often conflicting interests of their constituents, cultural influencers must navigate the complexities of identity and representation, and commercial influencers must balance the pursuit of profit with the need for ethical and sustainable practices. In each of these areas, the ability to influence effectively can determine the success or failure of an endeavor.

Chapter 2: The Political Landscape Politics is a field where influence is paramount. Political leaders, policymakers, and activists all rely on their ability to sway public opinion and garner support for their initiatives. The political landscape is shaped by a variety of factors, including ideology, partisanship, and the distribution of power. Understanding these dynamics is crucial for anyone seeking to navigate the world of politics effectively.

One of the key elements of political influence is the ability to build coalitions. Successful politicians understand that they cannot achieve their goals alone; they need the support of other leaders, interest groups, and the public. Building coalitions involves finding common ground, negotiating compromises, and fostering a sense of shared purpose. It requires strong interpersonal skills, strategic thinking, and the ability to communicate effectively with diverse audiences.

Another important aspect of political influence is the role of the media. The media serves as a conduit for political messages, shaping public perceptions and amplifying the voices of those in power. Politicians who can effectively manage their media presence—whether through traditional outlets like newspapers and television or newer platforms like social media—can significantly enhance their influence. This involves not only crafting compelling messages but also being able to respond quickly and effectively to criticism and crises.

Public opinion is another crucial factor in the political landscape. Politicians who can accurately gauge the mood of the electorate and align their messages with the values and concerns of their constituents are more likely to succeed. This requires a deep understanding of the social and cultural context in which political decisions are made, as well as the ability to conduct and interpret public opinion research. It also involves being attuned to the changing dynamics of political engagement, including the rise of grassroots movements and the increasing importance of digital activism.

Navigating the political landscape is a complex and challenging task, but it is also one that offers tremendous opportunities for those who can master the art of influence. By building coalitions, managing media presence, and understanding public opinion, political influencers can shape the direction of policy and governance in profound ways.

Chapter 3: Cultural Dynamics Culture is a powerful force that shapes our identities, values, and behaviors. Cultural influencers—whether they are artists, writers, entertainers, or activists—play a crucial role in shaping the narratives that define our societies. Navigating the world of culture requires a deep understanding of the diverse and dynamic nature of cultural expression, as well as the ability to connect with audiences on an emotional and intellectual level.

One of the key elements of cultural influence is authenticity. Cultural influencers who can authentically express their own experiences and perspectives are more likely to resonate with their audiences. This involves being true to oneself, embracing vulnerability, and sharing stories that reflect the complexities of the human experience. Authenticity fosters a sense of trust and connection, making it easier for cultural influencers to inspire and motivate their audiences.

Another important aspect of cultural influence is the ability to navigate the complexities of identity and representation. Cultural influencers must be mindful of the diverse identities and experiences that make up their audiences. This involves being aware of issues related to race, gender, sexuality, and other aspects of identity, and striving to create inclusive and equitable spaces. It also involves challenging stereotypes and advocating for greater representation and visibility for marginalized communities.

The power of storytelling is another crucial factor in cultural influence. Stories have the ability to convey complex ideas and emotions in a way that is accessible and relatable. Cultural influencers who can craft compelling narratives—whether through literature, film, music, or other forms of artistic expression—can shape the way people see the world and inspire them to take action. This requires not only creativity and imagination but also a deep understanding of the cultural and social context in which stories are told.

Navigating the cultural landscape is both a challenging and rewarding endeavor. By embracing authenticity, promoting inclusive representation, and harnessing the power of storytelling, cultural influencers can create meaningful connections with their audiences and drive positive social change.

Chapter 4: The Business of Influence Commerce is a field where influence can make or break a business. Business leaders, marketers, and entrepreneurs all rely on their ability to persuade customers, investors, and partners to support their ventures. Navigating the world of commerce requires a deep understanding of market dynamics, consumer behavior, and the principles of effective communication.

One of the key elements of business influence is brand building. A strong brand is one that is recognizable, trustworthy, and appealing to its target audience. Building a successful brand involves creating a clear and compelling identity, consistently delivering on promises, and fostering positive relationships with customers. It also involves being able to adapt and innovate in response to changing market conditions and consumer preferences.

Another important aspect of business influence is the ability to create value for customers. Successful businesses understand that their influence is built on the value they provide to their customers. This involves not only offering high-quality products and services but also creating positive and meaningful experiences for customers. It requires a deep understanding of customer needs and preferences, as well as the ability to engage with customers in a genuine and responsive manner.

The power of storytelling is also crucial in the business world. Just as in the cultural sphere, stories have the ability to convey complex ideas and emotions in a way that is accessible and relatable. Business leaders who can craft compelling narratives—whether about their brand, their products, or their mission—can create a deeper connection with their customers and inspire loyalty and advocacy. This involves not only creativity and imagination but also a strategic understanding of how to communicate effectively with different audiences.

Navigating the world of commerce is a challenging and dynamic task, but it is also one that offers tremendous opportunities for those who can master the art of influence. By building strong brands, creating value for customers, and harnessing the power of storytelling, business influencers can drive growth and success in their ventures.

Chapter 5: The Intersection of Politics and Culture The intersection of politics and culture is a dynamic and often contentious space. Political and cultural influencers alike must navigate the complex and ever-changing relationship between these two spheres. Understanding the ways in which politics and culture intersect can provide valuable insights for those seeking to influence change in either domain.

One of the key ways in which politics and culture intersect is through the shaping of national identity. Political leaders often use cultural symbols and narratives to create a sense of shared identity and purpose among their constituents. This can involve the promotion of certain values, traditions, and historical narratives that align with their political agenda. Cultural influencers, in turn, can use their platforms to challenge or reinforce these narratives, shaping the way people understand and relate to their national identity.

Another important aspect of the intersection of politics and culture is the role of cultural policy. Governments often enact policies that directly impact cultural production and expression. This can include funding for the arts, censorship and regulation of media, and the promotion of certain cultural industries. Understanding the ways in which cultural policy is shaped and implemented can provide valuable insights for those seeking to influence cultural production and expression.

The power of cultural activism is another crucial factor in the intersection of politics and culture. Cultural activists use their platforms to advocate for social and political change, often challenging dominant narratives and pushing for greater representation and equity. This involves not only creating compelling cultural works but also engaging in advocacy and activism to promote their causes. Cultural activists who can effectively navigate the political landscape and build coalitions with other activists and organizations can drive significant social and political change.

Navigating the intersection of politics and culture requires a nuanced understanding of the ways in which these two spheres influence and shape one another. By understanding the role of national identity, cultural policy, and cultural activism, political and cultural influencers can create meaningful change in both domains.

Chapter 6: The Intersection of Politics and Commerce The relationship between politics and commerce is complex and multifaceted. Political decisions and policies can have a significant impact on business operations, while commercial interests often shape political agendas. Understanding the ways in which politics and commerce intersect can provide valuable insights for those seeking to influence change in either domain.

One of the key ways in which politics and commerce intersect is through regulation.

One of the key ways in which politics and commerce intersect is through regulation. Governments create and enforce regulations that businesses must adhere to, covering everything from environmental standards to labor practices. These regulations can have significant impacts on business operations, influencing costs, market entry, and competitiveness. Businesses that can effectively navigate regulatory landscapes can gain a competitive advantage, while those that struggle with compliance may face fines, legal challenges, and reputational damage.

Another important aspect of the intersection of politics and commerce is the role of lobbying and advocacy. Businesses often seek to influence political decisions that affect their interests by lobbying policymakers, funding political campaigns, and engaging in advocacy efforts. This involves building relationships with key stakeholders, presenting compelling arguments, and mobilizing support from other businesses and interest groups. Effective lobbying can result in favorable policies and regulations, while ineffective efforts can lead to missed opportunities and potential backlash.

The impact of political stability on commerce is another crucial factor. Political stability—or the lack thereof—can significantly affect business operations and investment decisions. In stable political environments, businesses can plan and invest with greater confidence, knowing that policies and regulations are unlikely to change abruptly. In contrast, political instability can create uncertainty and risk, leading businesses to delay or cancel investments, seek alternative markets, or implement contingency plans. Understanding the political climate and being able to adapt to changing conditions are essential skills for business leaders.

Navigating the intersection of politics and commerce requires a strategic understanding of both fields. By effectively managing regulatory compliance, engaging in lobbying and advocacy, and adapting to political stability, businesses can enhance their influence and drive success in their ventures.

Chapter 7: The Intersection of Culture and Commerce The relationship between culture and commerce is rich and multifaceted. Cultural products and experiences—such as music, film, fashion, and art—drive economic activity and shape consumer behavior. At the same time, commercial interests often influence cultural production and expression. Understanding the ways in which culture and commerce intersect can provide valuable insights for those seeking to influence change in either domain.

One of the key ways in which culture and commerce intersect is through the concept of cultural branding. Cultural branding involves leveraging cultural symbols, narratives, and identities to create a strong and resonant brand. Successful cultural brands are those that can tap into the cultural zeitgeist, reflecting and shaping the values and aspirations of their target audience. This involves not only creating appealing products and experiences but also fostering a sense of community and belonging around the brand.

Another important aspect of the intersection of culture and commerce is the role of intellectual property. Intellectual property laws protect the rights of creators and innovators, allowing them to monetize their cultural products and experiences. This includes copyright for creative works, trademarks for brand identities, and patents for inventions. Understanding and navigating intellectual property laws is essential for cultural producers and businesses seeking to protect and capitalize on their creations.

The impact of cultural trends on consumer behavior is another crucial factor. Cultural trends—such as shifts in fashion, music, or entertainment—can significantly influence consumer preferences and purchasing decisions. Businesses that can identify and respond to cultural trends can gain a competitive advantage, while those that fail to do so may struggle to stay relevant. This involves not only staying attuned to cultural developments but also being able to adapt and innovate in response to changing tastes and preferences.

Navigating the intersection of culture and commerce requires a strategic understanding of both fields. By leveraging cultural branding, protecting intellectual property, and responding to cultural trends, businesses can enhance their influence and drive success in the cultural economy.

Chapter 8: Strategies for Effective Influence Influence is an art that requires a combination of skills, strategies, and insights. Whether in the realms of politics, culture, or commerce, effective influencers are those who can build credibility, connect with their audience, and inspire action. Understanding and applying key strategies for influence can enhance one's ability to drive change and achieve goals.

One of the key strategies for effective influence is the art of storytelling. Stories have the power to convey complex ideas, evoke emotions, and create a sense of connection. Influencers who can craft compelling narratives—whether about their vision, their values, or their achievements—can create a deeper and more lasting impact. This involves not only creativity and imagination but also the ability to understand and address the needs and concerns of the audience.

Another important strategy for effective influence is the use of social proof. Social proof is the idea that people are more likely to adopt a behavior or belief if they see others doing the same. Influencers who can leverage social proof—whether through testimonials, endorsements, or social media engagement—

can enhance their credibility and persuade others to follow their lead. This involves not only building a strong network of supporters but also showcasing their support in a visible and impactful way.

The power of empathy is another crucial factor in effective influence. Empathy involves understanding and sharing the feelings of others, creating a sense of connection and trust. Influencers who can demonstrate empathy—whether through active listening, compassionate communication, or genuine concern for others—can build stronger relationships and inspire greater loyalty and support. This requires not only emotional intelligence but also the ability to create a safe and inclusive environment for all.

Navigating the art of influence requires a combination of skills, strategies, and insights. By mastering the art of storytelling, leveraging social proof, and demonstrating empathy, influencers can enhance their ability to drive change and achieve their goals.

Chapter 9: Ethical Considerations Influence is a powerful tool, and with great power comes great responsibility. Ethical considerations are crucial for anyone seeking to navigate the intersection of politics, culture, and commerce. Understanding and applying ethical principles can help ensure that influence is used in a way that is respectful, fair, and beneficial to all.

One of the key ethical considerations in the realm of influence is transparency. Transparency involves being open and honest about one's intentions, actions, and outcomes. Influencers who can demonstrate transparency—whether through clear communication, accountability, or ethical conduct—can build trust and credibility with their audience. This requires not only a commitment to honesty but also a willingness to acknowledge and address mistakes and challenges.

Another important ethical consideration is the principle of respect. Respect involves recognizing and valuing the dignity and rights of others. Influencers who can demonstrate respect—whether through inclusive representation, compassionate communication, or fair treatment—can create a positive and supportive environment for all. This requires not only a commitment to equity and inclusion but also a willingness to challenge and address discrimination and bias.

The impact of influence on vulnerable populations is another crucial ethical consideration. Vulnerable populations—such as marginalized communities, children, or those experiencing hardship—may be particularly susceptible to the effects of influence. Influencers who can demonstrate a commitment to protecting and empowering vulnerable populations—whether through ethical advocacy, responsible messaging, or compassionate action—can create a positive and lasting impact. This requires not only a commitment to social justice but also a willingness to listen to and amplify the voices of those who are most affected.

Navigating the ethical considerations of influence requires a commitment to transparency, respect, and social responsibility. By applying these principles, influencers can ensure that their actions are ethical and beneficial to all.

Chapter 10: Case Studies of Influence Examining real-world examples of influence can provide valuable insights and lessons for those seeking to navigate the intersection of politics, culture, and commerce. Case studies of successful influencers—whether in the realms of politics, culture, or commerce—can highlight the strategies and principles that contribute to effective influence.

One notable case study is the influence of Nelson Mandela in the realm of politics. Mandela's leadership in the anti-apartheid movement and his efforts to promote reconciliation and social justice in South Africa are widely recognized as examples of effective political influence. Mandela's ability to build coalitions, communicate a compelling vision, and demonstrate empathy and resilience were key factors in his success. His legacy continues to inspire political influencers around the world.

Another important case study is the influence of Beyoncé in the realm of culture. Beyoncé's impact on music, fashion, and social justice has made her one of the most influential cultural figures of our time. Beyoncé's ability to leverage her platform for advocacy, create compelling narratives, and promote inclusive representation has been key to her influence. Her work continues to shape the cultural landscape and inspire other cultural influencers.

In the realm of commerce, the influence of Steve Jobs is a notable case study. Jobs' leadership at Apple and his impact on technology and innovation are widely recognized as examples of effective business influence. Jobs' ability to build a strong brand, create value for customers, and tell compelling stories about his products and vision were key factors in his success. His legacy continues to influence business leaders and entrepreneurs around the world.

Examining these and other case studies of influence can provide valuable insights and lessons for those seeking to navigate the intersection of politics, culture, and commerce. By understanding the strategies and principles that contribute to effective influence, individuals can enhance their own ability to drive change and achieve their goals.

Chapter 11: Future Trends in Influence The landscape of influence is constantly evolving, shaped by technological advancements, cultural shifts, and political developments. Understanding the future trends in influence can provide valuable insights for those seeking to stay ahead of the curve and navigate the intersection of politics, culture, and commerce effectively.

One of the key future trends in influence is the rise of digital and social media. Digital and social media platforms have revolutionized the way people communicate, share information, and build communities. Influencers who can effectively leverage these platforms—whether through social media engagement, digital storytelling, or online advocacy—can enhance their reach and impact. This requires not only a deep understanding of digital media but also the ability to adapt and innovate in response to changing technologies and trends.

Another important future trend is the growing importance of data and analytics. Data and analytics provide valuable insights into audience behavior, preferences, and trends. Influencers who can effectively use data and analytics—whether through audience segmentation, targeted messaging, or performance measurement—can enhance their ability to connect with their audience and achieve their goals. This requires not only technical skills but also This requires not only technical skills but also the ability to interpret and act on data insights effectively.

The impact of globalization is another crucial future trend. Globalization has interconnected markets, cultures, and political systems, creating both opportunities and challenges for influencers. Influencers who can navigate the complexities of a globalized world—whether through cross-cultural communication, global partnerships, or international advocacy—can enhance their reach and impact. This involves not only understanding different cultural contexts but also being able to adapt and innovate in response to global trends and developments.

The rise of ethical and sustainable practices is another important future trend. Increasingly, consumers, voters, and audiences are demanding ethical and sustainable practices from businesses, politicians, and cultural influencers. Those who can demonstrate a commitment to social responsibility—whether through ethical production, transparent governance, or inclusive representation—can build trust and loyalty with their audience. This requires not only a commitment to ethical principles but also the ability to communicate and act on these principles effectively.

Navigating the future trends in influence requires a combination of skills, strategies, and insights. By leveraging digital and social media, using data and analytics, navigating globalization, and embracing ethical and sustainable practices, influencers can stay ahead of the curve and drive positive change in the interconnected world.

Chapter 12: The Path Forward The path forward for anyone seeking to navigate the intersection of politics, culture, and commerce is both challenging and rewarding. It requires a deep understanding of the dynamics of influence, a commitment to ethical principles, and the ability to adapt and innovate in response to changing conditions. By mastering the art of influence, individuals can drive meaningful change and achieve their goals.

One of the key elements of the path forward is continuous learning. The landscape of influence is constantly evolving, and staying ahead of the curve requires a commitment to ongoing education and growth. This involves not only staying informed about developments in politics, culture, and commerce but also seeking out new skills and perspectives. Continuous learning fosters adaptability and innovation, essential qualities for effective influencers.

Another important element of the path forward is collaboration. Influence is often most effective when it is a collective effort, involving the contributions and support of others. Building strong networks, fostering partnerships, and engaging in collaborative initiatives can enhance one's ability to drive change and achieve goals. Collaboration involves not only building relationships but also creating a sense of shared purpose and mutual support.

The power of resilience is another crucial factor in the path forward. The journey of influence is often fraught with challenges, setbacks, and obstacles. Those who can demonstrate resilience—whether through perseverance, adaptability, or a positive mindset—can navigate these challenges and continue to move forward. Resilience involves not only the ability to bounce back from setbacks but also the ability to learn and grow from them.

Navigating the path forward requires a combination of continuous learning, collaboration, and resilience. By embracing these principles, individuals can enhance their ability to influence and drive meaningful change in the interconnected world.

Chapter 13: Building and Maintaining Credibility Credibility is the cornerstone of influence. Without it, even the most compelling messages and strategies will fall flat. Credibility is built on a foundation of trust, reliability, and expertise. Influencers who can demonstrate these qualities are more likely to earn the respect and loyalty of their audience.

One of the key ways to build credibility is through expertise. Demonstrating a deep and nuanced understanding of one's field—whether it is politics, culture, or commerce—can establish an influencer as a knowledgeable and reliable source. This involves not only acquiring knowledge and skills but also sharing them in a way that is accessible and valuable to others. Thought leadership, through writing, speaking, and teaching, can enhance an influencer's credibility and authority.

Another important aspect of credibility is consistency. Consistently delivering on promises, maintaining high standards of conduct, and aligning actions with values can build trust and reliability. This requires not only a commitment to integrity but also the ability to communicate transparently and respond to challenges and criticisms effectively. Consistency fosters a sense of trust and reliability, making it easier for influencers to persuade and inspire their audience.

The role of authenticity in building credibility cannot be overstated. Authenticity involves being true to oneself and one's values, sharing genuine experiences and perspectives, and demonstrating vulnerability and empathy. Authentic influencers are those who can create a sense of connection and trust with their audience, making it easier to inspire and motivate action. This requires not only self-awareness and confidence but also the ability to communicate and engage with others in a genuine and compassionate manner.

Building and maintaining credibility is an ongoing process that requires a combination of expertise, consistency, and authenticity. By demonstrating these qualities, influencers can enhance their ability to drive change and achieve their goals.

Chapter 14: The Role of Innovation Innovation is a key driver of influence in the interconnected world. Whether in the realms of politics, culture, or commerce, the ability to innovate can set influencers apart and create new opportunities for impact. Understanding and leveraging the principles of innovation can enhance one's ability to navigate the complex and dynamic landscape of influence.

One of the key principles of innovation is creativity. Creativity involves generating new ideas, exploring unconventional solutions, and challenging the status quo. Influencers who can harness their creativity—whether through artistic expression, problem-solving, or strategic thinking—can create unique and compelling visions that resonate with their audience. This requires not only imagination and curiosity but also the ability to take risks and embrace failure as a learning opportunity.

Another important principle of innovation is collaboration. Innovation often thrives in environments where diverse perspectives and skills can come together to create something new. Influencers who can foster a culture of collaboration—whether within their teams, organizations, or communities—can enhance their ability to innovate and drive change. This involves not only building strong relationships but also creating a sense of shared purpose and mutual support.

CHAPTER 1

The role of technology in innovation cannot be overlooked. Technological advancements—such as artificial intelligence, digital media, and blockchain—are transforming the way people communicate, create, and engage with the world. Influencers who can leverage these technologies to enhance their impact can stay ahead of the curve and create new opportunities for influence. This requires not only technical skills but also the ability to adapt and innovate in response to changing technologies and trends.

Innovation is a key driver of influence in the interconnected world. By harnessing creativity, fostering collaboration, and leveraging technology, influencers can enhance their ability to drive change and achieve their goals.

2

Chapter 15: The Power of Networks

Networks are a crucial element of influence in the interconnected world. Whether in the realms of politics, culture, or commerce, the ability to build and leverage networks can enhance one's reach, credibility, and impact. Understanding and applying the principles of networking can enhance one's ability to navigate the complex and dynamic landscape of influence.

One of the key principles of networking is relationship-building. Building strong and meaningful relationships with key stakeholders—whether they are colleagues, partners, or supporters—can enhance an influencer's ability to achieve their goals. This involves not only building rapport and trust but also demonstrating genuine interest and support for others. Relationship-building fosters a sense of community and mutual support, making it easier to mobilize resources and garner support for one's initiatives.

Another important principle of networking is reciprocity. Reciprocity involves the mutual exchange of support, resources, and opportunities. Influencers who can demonstrate a commitment to reciprocity—whether through mentoring, collaboration, or advocacy—can enhance their ability to build and leverage networks. This requires not only a willingness to give and receive support but also the ability to create a culture of mutual benefit and cooperation.

The power of digital networks cannot be overlooked. Digital and social media platforms have revolutionized the way people connect, share information, and build communities. Influencers who can effectively leverage digital networks—whether through social media engagement, online communities, or digital advocacy—can enhance their reach and impact. This requires not only a deep understanding of digital media but also the ability to adapt and innovate in response to changing technologies and trends.

Networks are a crucial element of influence in the interconnected world. By building strong relationships, demonstrating reciprocity, and leveraging digital networks, influencers can enhance their ability to drive change and achieve their goals.

3

Chapter 16: The Art of Negotiation

Negotiation is a key skill for anyone seeking to navigate the intersection of politics, culture, and commerce. Whether in the realms of policy-making, cultural production, or business transactions, the ability to negotiate effectively can enhance one's ability to achieve desired outcomes and build positive relationships. Understanding and applying the principles of negotiation can enhance one's ability to drive change and achieve goals.

One of the key principles of negotiation is preparation. Effective negotiators are those who come to the table well-prepared, with a clear understanding of their goals, interests, and priorities. This involves not only researching and gathering information but also anticipating potential challenges and objections. Preparation fosters confidence and clarity, making it easier to navigate the negotiation process and achieve desired outcomes.

Another important principle of negotiation is communication. Negotiation involves not only articulating one's own interests and goals but also actively listening to and understanding the interests and goals of others. Effective communication—whether through persuasive arguments, active listening, or empathetic engagement—can enhance one's ability to build rapport, find common ground, and negotiate mutually beneficial agreements. This requires not only strong communication skills but also the ability to adapt and respond to different communication styles and preferences.

CHAPTER 16: THE ART OF NEGOTIATION

The role of creativity in negotiation cannot be overlooked. Creative problem-solving involves generating and exploring new and unconventional solutions that can satisfy the interests and goals of all parties involved. Influencers who can demonstrate creativity in negotiation—whether through brainstorming, collaboration, or strategic thinking—can enhance their ability to find innovative and mutually beneficial solutions. This requires not only imagination and flexibility but also the ability to take risks and embrace uncertainty.

Negotiation is a key skill for anyone seeking to navigate the intersection of politics, culture, and commerce. By preparing effectively, communicating persuasively, and demonstrating creativity, influencers can enhance their ability to drive change and achieve their goals.

4

Chapter 17: The Legacy of Influence

The legacy of influence is the lasting impact that individuals and organizations leave on the world. Whether in the realms of politics, culture, or commerce, the ability to create a positive and lasting legacy is a key measure of success. Understanding and applying the principles of legacy-building can enhance one's ability to drive meaningful change and leave a lasting impact.

One of the key principles of legacy-building is vision. A compelling vision is one that articulates a clear and inspiring goal for the future. Influencers who can craft and communicate a compelling vision—whether for their community, organization, or cause—can inspire and mobilize others to work towards that goal. This involves not only imagination and strategic thinking but also the ability to communicate and engage with others in a way that resonates with their values and aspirations.

Another important principle of legacy-building is impact. Impact involves creating positive and meaningful change that benefits others and contributes to the greater good. Influencers who can demonstrate a commitment to impact—whether through social, cultural, or economic initiatives—can enhance their ability to leave a lasting legacy. This requires not only a deep understanding of the needs and challenges of others but also the ability to implement and sustain impactful initiatives.

The role of mentorship in legacy-building cannot be overlooked. Men-

CHAPTER 17: THE LEGACY OF INFLUENCE

torship involves guiding, supporting, and empowering others to achieve their goals and realize their potential. Influencers who can demonstrate a commitment to mentorship—whether through formal programs, informal relationships, or community engagement—can enhance their ability to leave a lasting legacy. This requires not only a willingness to share knowledge and experience but also the ability to create a culture of mutual support and growth.

The legacy of influence is the lasting impact that individuals and organizations leave on the world. By crafting a compelling vision, creating positive impact, and demonstrating a commitment to mentorship, influencers can enhance their ability to drive meaningful change and leave a lasting legacy.

"Blueprint of Influence: Navigating the Intersection of Politics, Culture, and Commerce"

In a world where the lines between politics, culture, and commerce blur, understanding the dynamics of influence is paramount. **"Blueprint of Influence: Navigating the Intersection of Politics, Culture, and Commerce"** dives deep into the art and science of shaping opinions, driving change, and achieving success across these interconnected spheres.

This comprehensive guide explores the foundational principles of influence, from building credibility and harnessing emotional appeal to leveraging social proof. It delves into the intricate political landscape, examining the power of coalitions, media presence, and public opinion. The cultural dynamics of authenticity, representation, and storytelling are unpacked, highlighting the role of cultural influencers in shaping societal narratives.

The book also sheds light on the business of influence, emphasizing brand building, creating customer value, and the critical role of storytelling in commerce. As readers journey through the pages, they will discover the intersections of politics and culture, politics and commerce, and culture and commerce, gaining valuable insights into the complex relationships that drive change.

Practical strategies for effective influence, ethical considerations, and real-world case studies provide readers with actionable tools and lessons. The book also looks ahead, identifying future trends in influence, from the rise of digital media to the importance of data analytics and ethical practices.

"Blueprint of Influence" is an essential read for anyone looking to master the art of influence and make a lasting impact in today's interconnected world. Whether you're a political leader, cultural influencer, or business entrepreneur, this book offers the insights and strategies you need to navigate the complex landscape of influence and drive meaningful change.

www.ingramcontent.com/pod-product-compliance
Lightning Source LLC
LaVergne TN
LVHW020508080526
838202LV00057B/6232